Is Somewhere Always Far Away?

POEMS ABOUT PLACES

Leland B. Jacobs
Pictures by Jeff Kaufman

A Bill Martin Book

HENRY HOLT AND COMPANY ▪ NEW YORK

SE

Bill Martin Jr, Ph.D., has devoted his life to the education of young children.
Bill Martin Books reflect his philosophy: that children's imaginations
are opened up through the play of language, the imagery of illustration,
and the permanent joy of reading books.

j808.1
J15i

For my favorite J's:
   A.D.J.
   K.D.J.
   J.K.J.
   and
   B.H.J.
        —L.B.J.

For Micah, Naomi, McCoy, and Alec
        —J.K.

Henry Holt and Company, Inc. / *Publishers since 1866*
115 West 18th Street, New York, New York 10011

Henry Holt is a registered trademark of Henry Holt and Company, Inc.

Text copyright © 1993 by Allan D. Jacobs
Illustrations copyright © 1993 by Jeff Kaufman
All rights reserved.
Published in Canada by Fitzhenry & Whiteside Ltd., 91 Granton Drive, Richmond Hill, Ontario L4B 2N5.
Originally published in slightly different form in 1967 by Holt, Rinehart and Winston,
with illustrations by John E. Johnson.

A CIP catalog record for this book is available from the Library of Congress.

ISBN 0-8050-2677-0

First Edition—1993

Printed in the United States of America on acid-free paper.∞

10 9 8 7 6 5 4 3 2 1

KN   FEB   '94

Contents

Somewhere

Where, oh where,
Can somewhere be?
In outer space?
Beneath the sea?

Is somewhere
Always far away?
In other lands?
Beyond today?

Is somewhere
Always farther still?
Beyond the woods,
Beyond the hill?

It's difficult
To be aware
Of somewhere else
Until you're there.

COUN

The Little Road

The highway shouted, "Straight ahead."
The little road said, "Turn!
I'll show you how a brook runs,
Banked by flowers and fern."

The highway pushed on straight ahead.
The little road led right,
"I'll take you through the cool woods
With birches silvery white."

**NEXT EXIT
70 MILES**

TRY

The highway beckoned straight ahead.
The little road said, "Here,
I'll lead you where the birds nest,
Where rabbits live, and deer."

The highway hurried straight ahead.
The little roadway crept,
And everywhere, abundantly,
Its promises it kept.

'Hopper and 'Pillar

A grasshopper said
To a caterpillar furry,
"I can't wait for you.
I'm really in a hurry."

The caterpillar said
To the grasshopper green,
"I'm really not the type
For a flying machine."

So the 'hopper hurried
While the 'pillar went slow,
And they both got to where
They wanted to go.

Waves

Little lake waves ripple in
    And gently pat the land.
Ocean waves toss boldly
    And slap the rocks and sand.

Lake waves have a pleasant way
    Of skipping up to shore,
While ocean waves are arrogant—
    They push and rush and roar.

Lake waves are playful waves,
    They have a tickly reach,
But ocean waves are rowdy waves
    That chase me up the beach.

A Rooster Singing

The rooster crows and flaps
    his wings—
He wants attention when he
    sings.
He struts and scratches with
    his feet
To say he thinks his song is
    sweet.

So, when he crows with all
    his might,
Although his singing is a
    fright,
I listen, just to be polite.

The Bee

Out in our garden lives a bee,
An energetic fellow, he—
    Buzz-buzz-buzz—
Dips into our flowers, and then,
Dips into each one again,
    Buzz-buzz-buzz.
A busier bee there never was,
All work, work, work, and
    Buzz-buzz-buzz.

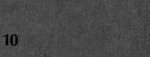

10

Duet

I sang my song to a chickadee,
    But he was busy eating,
I sang my song to a little lamb,
    But he was busy bleating.
I sang my song to a yellow
        chick,
    But he was busy peeping,
I sang my song to a puppy dog.
    But he was busy sleeping.
I sang my song to myself, I thought,
    All in the windy weather,
But a little breeze picked up
      the tune,
    And so we sang together.

Perhaps

Could we go to the circus?
    Could we go to the park?
May I play outdoors
    Until it's dark?
        "Perhaps," they say
      In the nicest way.

T Y

May I have some popcorn?
    May I have a sweet?
May I take my lunch
    Outdoors to eat?
        "Perhaps," they say
        In a pleasant way.

Could we all dress up
    And have a show?
And does "Perhaps"
    Mean "Yes" or "No"?
        "Maybe," they say
        In a "Perhaps" way.

Bus Stop

The bus stop is a special place.
Of that there is no doubt.
A yellow line tells common cars
That they must all stay out.

The bus stop is a special spot.
Of that it's very clear.
A sign in flaming red declares
There is "NO PARKING HERE."

While other cars
      must cruise around
To find a parking space,
A bus must feel
      like royalty
To have its special
      place.

City Pigeons

In Herald Square,
In Herald Square,
I saw the pigeons gathered there,
Talking, strutting with an air
As if they owned all Herald Square,
Standing on the hot concrete,
Having little snacks to eat.
      And I'd call
      To your attention,
      The pigeons hold
      A huge convention
            There
In Herald Square,
In Herald Square.

The Subway Train

The subway train, the
      subway train,
If you'll permit me to explain,
Is like a busy beetle black
That scoots along a silver track;
And, whether it be night or day,
The beetle has to light its way,
Because the only place it's found
Is deep, deep, deep, deep,
      underground.

Mr. Giraffe

Mr. Giraffe,
You make me laugh
Whenever I come to the zoo.
You never smile
Like the crocodile
Or grin, like the lions do.

Mr. Giraffe,
Excuse my laugh,
For I think you're really fine.
Though the crocodile
And the lions smile,
They are no friends of mine.

The Bridge

What stands firm upon the ground?
The tall and sturdy gray bridge.

What stands ready all year round?
The faithful night–and–day bridge.

What stands reaching toward the sun?
The mighty, towering, strong bridge.

What stands welcoming everyone?
The busy–all–day–long bridge.

What stands safe from waters blue?
The reaching–for–the–sky bridge.

What stands waiting just for you?
The quick–cross–over high bridge.

BELIEVE

The High-Stepping Man

There once was a man
   Who stepped so high
His knees touched the treetops,
   His head touched the sky.

He stepped over mountains
   And housetops and hills;
He stepped over flagpoles
   And factories and mills.

This man of the high step
   Drew curious crowds
Which he never saw
   With his head in the clouds.

With his head in the clouds,
   How could he know
Just what was down
   Where his feet had to go?

The high-stepping man
   Is with us no more,
For he couldn't tell
   That he'd come to the shore.

How sad for the man
   With that high-stepping knee!
He stepped in the ocean
   And sank in the sea.

At the Store

A lady cat once kept a store.
  Her store was just for kittens.
Now, what do you think the kittens bought?
  Calico for mittens,
Bright ribbons for around their necks,
  And catnip sweets for chewing,
And little cans of fish for lunch,
  And books to study mewing.

Like a Fly

Many's the time
I've wished that I
Could walk the ceiling
Like a fly.

I'd walk the ceiling
Safe and free
And look below
Where I could see

My toys and books.
And then I'd sit
And feel all upside
Down a bit.

Wishing

I wish I had a kitten,
I wish I had a dog,
I wish I had a crocodile,
Or a pollywog.

I wish I had a magic hat,
A magic cloak and stick,
I wish I had an uncle
Who could do a magic trick.

I wish I had a sailing ship
That had a jolly crew—
I wish I had a wish, for once,
That really would come true.

The Choice

What shall we buy to eat on our bread?
"Smooth golden honey," Marilyn said.
"Wait!" cried Robin. "Let's have jam!"
"Marmalade! Marmalade!" called out Sam.
"Sugar?" asked Amy. "Oh, no! Please,"
Tim protested, "I want cheese!"
"We must have butter," Mother said.
So we had butter on our bread.

22

Shoelaces

Although I've tried and
    tried and tried,
I cannot keep my laces
    tied.
I really don't know what to
    do—

Unless I stick them
    tied with glue—
Except that such a
    sticky mess
Would not be good for
    shoes, I guess.

Keepsakes

I keep bottle caps,
    I keep strings,
I keep keys and corks
    And all such things.

When people say,
"What good are they?"
The answer's hard to get
For just how I will use them all
I don't know yet.

The Secret

A secret! A secret!
I just heard a secret
And nobody else must hear.
   No talking!
   No telling!
   No whispering!
   No hinting!
Or a secret will disappear.

A secret! A secret!
I just heard a secret!
Must it be kept so well?
   A week?
   An hour?
   A minute?
   A second?
I'm afraid I'm going to tell.

My Legs and I

I say to my legs,
  "Legs," I say,
"Let's go out
  To run and play."

So off we go,
  My legs and I,
Skipping, romping,
  Jumping high.

28

Then I say to my legs,
    "Legs," I say,
"I'm much too tired
    To run and play."

So legs and I
    Toward home we go,
Walking, walking,
    Slow, slow, slow.

How Quiet?

They said I must be quiet,
So how quiet shall I be?
Quiet as a snowflake?
Quiet as a flea?
Quiet as a dandelion?
Quiet as the sun?
Since I have to be so quiet,
Which would be most fun?

Not Tonight

"No. Not tonight.
It's too late. No."
These are the night words
Big folks know.

When I grow up,
I'll clearly state,
"Don't go to bed yet,
It's not late."

"Stay up longer—
Sing and play."
That's what I
Am going to say.

Night

I wrapped the night around me—
Velvet black, a cloak it made,
With silver stars for buttons…
I drew the cloak around me, unafraid.

I wrapped the night around me—
Velvet black, that shimmered as I swept
Around the moonlit room.
And in the furry feel of night I slept.